Cover Illustrator
Summer Scharringhausen

Editor
Katie Rivera

Copyright © 2023 by Michael A. Rivera Jr.

All rights reserved. No part of this publication may be reproduced, distributed, or transmitted in any form or by any means, including photocopying, recording, or other electronic or mechanical methods, without the prior written permission of the author, except in the case of brief quotations embodied in critical reviews and certain other noncommercial uses permitted by copyright law. For permission requests, Email the author, subject "Attention: Permissions Coordinator," at the Email address below.

focusandvision@gmail.com
Or
https://www.focusandvisionministries.com/store

Ordering Information:
Quantity sales: Special discounts are available on quantity purchases by corporations, associations, and others. For details, contact the author at focusandvision@gmail.com.

Orders by U.S. trade bookstores and wholesalers. Please contact your distribution channel or the author at the Email address above.

The Word of the Day: Because One Word Can Change Your Life (Alpha)

ISBN: 978-1-63553-011-7
ISBN ebook: 978-1-63553-008-7

1. The main category of the book - Religion
2. The second category of the book - Spirituality

First Edition

About the Author

by Bruce Clark

It all started with an awkward classroom entrance passage at a school open house. Two dads trying to navigate both the less-than-adequate physical space, but also the promise of new possibilities for our daughters as they anticipated kindergarten. Little did we realize then that our daughters would become fast and best friends, and that we too would glimpse a spark in the other in that briefest of pleasant exchanges. Michael has a welcoming and earnest smile that met me that August night, and I sensed immediately that there was an approachability and a depth to his presence. I find this to be consistent with the man that he is, the man that stands behind these pages: earnestness and warmth. Michael exudes a confidence in who he is as a man in pursuit of His God through His word. He is a man who has been crafted in the crucible of military experience, where the chain of command and the following of orders is vital to the backbone of a well-functioning military. Until you understand that, Michael might seem a radical man when he answers a simple question of "So, what brings you to the community?" with an equally simple but challenging response of, "Because God sent us here."

He says such things like that so matter-of-factly, that one might wonder if he is joking with you, until you soon realize that he is not. When it comes to the things of God, Michael does not joke. That is one of his strengths: a guileless integrity that you, as a fellow in Christ, need to know. Because when you are in the heat of battle (and you ARE), you need to know who has your back. He is, as the famed Roman centurion who was the only person who Jesus marveled at, a man under orders. His faith is an expressed faith. His words are derived from experience: experience in life, experience in the presence of God, and experience in the word. "Study to shew yourself approved unto God, a workman that does not need to be ashamed, rightly dividing the word of truth." (2 Timothy 2:15). This devotional guide is an extension of that work that Michael cultivates daily in his life and in his practice.

AFFIRMATIONS FOR THE WORD OF THE DAY

I really enjoy the Focus and Vision "Word of the Day" and other ministry training. I look forward to receiving it each morning as an "aha" moment to my day. I even quote it from time to time in my sermons.

Dr. Paul Marzahn
Founding Pastor CROSSROADS CHURCH Lakeville, MN
Church planter and mentor
Community leader and developer

"Winsome, welcoming, and wise. The Word of the Day reflections from Rev. Michael Rivera offer the reader a brief daily dose of inspiration and insight. Anchoring himself on carefully and playfully chosen vocabulary, he pairs a word with each day of the year, allowing the word chosen to speak in turn its own words to any who would pause to listen and consider. If you are looking for a daily Christian devotion, or perhaps a simple conversation starter in a small group context, Rivera's Word of the Day might be just the resource you need."

Ryan McDaniel
CH (Maj) ILANG

"The words of the day that you send often directly relate to my struggles that week! The teachings you share guide me in both personal and professional relationships as well as guide me in my thought processes and help me stay resilient in these crazy times! Thank you for your consistency and constant compassion!"

Katia Campos
SrA ILANG

"Words do make a difference. Words can help build up a person and words can tear down a person. When I was a child, I grew up with adults telling me, "sticks and stones may break your bones, but names can never hurt you," when another child would call me names, or made fun of how I looked. As an adult, I know how a well-placed word can make a positive difference in a person's life, relationships, and livelihood. And there is no better word than words from God's Word. Michael Rivera does a masterful job of interpreting a Word from God and applying that word to our life situation. My prayer is that all who read this book are refreshed and empowered to continue your work for the Glory of God."

Rev. David Terrinoni
Retired U.S. Air Force Chaplain

"Thank you for the hundredth time for continuing to send the Word of the Day to me. While being away from my family, and with all the changes that have occurred around the world, reading "The Word of the Day" was one of the few uplifting consistencies in my life. Every day, I smiled to see how God was going to speak to me, and it always amazed me how often it was a Word I really needed to hear that day. The bible verses are a great addition to "The Word of the Day" because it shows how to implement God's words and reading the word helped me focus on what changes I needed to make, "The Word of the Day" was extremely important to me during my activation but what was great about it was my wife enjoyed reading it daily as well. "The Word of the Day" was a great way to still feel connected during our time of being separated."

Jason Erlick
TSgt ILANG

"Michael Rivera's daily devotion is inspiring, engaging, and thoughtful. I appreciate his authentic voice and delivery which allows the readers to reflect with Scriptures while challenging one's faith toward spiritual growth."

Lou Foyou
CH (MAJ) US Army

"The Word of the Day comes at the perfect time. Each day once the word is received, it finds a way to describe how your day is going or how it has been. Each scripture provided gives a Biblical description and shows how God plays a role in one's life daily. Thank you for providing me with "the word of the day" daily Chap!"

Logan Davis
SGT ILARNG

"Thanks for the Word! I first became a regular reader of Michael Rivera's Word of the Day while serving with the author as chaplains in National Guard COVID-19 response Operations. His challenging and inspirational messages caught on like wildfire and became a hopeful anticipation for our troops' daily morale. Soon over 600 team members were quizzing one another on the word and its life application. Even after completing our military mission that summer, our troops continue to request and discuss the Word of the Day by group messaging. I highly recommend this collection of daily devotions for personal and professional development individually or with groups."

Rev. Dr. Michael C. Doan, D.Min.,
BCC Chaplain, Lt Col USAF

Contents

Introduction		KNOW	33
CHRISTIAN	1	MOUNTAINTOP	35
WHO	3	RUN	37
RELATIONSHIPS	5	TRUST	39
SENT	7	WAITING	41
WORK	9	THANKFULNESS	43
PRAISE	11	WEAKNESS	45
OBEDIENCE	13	STAMINA	47
SPIRIT	15	FOCUS	49
SERVE	17	PERSPECTIVE	51
PRAYER	19	HAPHAZARD	53
LABORERS	21	RELAX	55
PROVISION	23	STILLNESS	57
BATTLE	25	CONFLICT	59
LIVE	27	REPENTANCE	61
THINK	29	References	
PRAY	31	Acknowledgements	

INTRODUCTION

Words are important! One word heard, read, or spoken at just the right time or place introduces and invites anyone to a new or different perspective. I have been called and chosen to use the power of a "word" to encourage and inspire all who read it. The content of this devotional began over ten years ago but did not take shape and fully come alive until the Winter of 2019. The intent and purpose of these writings is to motivate, inspire, encourage and challenge its reader. This book gets its title, The Word of the Day, from the arduous training and preparation I received at the United States Army Chaplain Center and School, where we were expected to always be prepared to deliver "a word" to sure up the mental and spiritual health of Soldiers in garrison and abroad. As a chaplain, I may only get three minutes in a day to speak into the life of those men and women under my care. I quickly realized the value of those three minutes. I set out to deliver a message that would be "Applicable to their real-life situations, brief enough to remember and Clear enough to capture their interest at first glance".

When time permits, I can use the scripture that follows "The Word of the Day" as the basis for a sermon at any time. Today, it continues to be a vital part of my ministry: civilian and military. My hope and prayer is that the "Word of the Day", God's Word, finds you wherever you are in life's journey and draws you closer to Him!

THE WORD OF THE DAY IS "CHRISTIAN"

A Christian is one who believes and follows the teachings of Jesus Christ. Christ met people where they were in life. Some were prostitutes, some hungry, some sick, some murderers, some drunks, some homeless and some adulterers. Being Christian has nothing to do with individual perspective, social status, financial standing or political party. A Christian is committed to unconditional love, forgiveness and compassion for others. Jesus consistently and continuously shows up in the least likely places, at the most appropriate time! If one is not careful, one might just miss Him. The evidence of your claim as being Christian will be evident in your treatment of all people, everywhere. If you are gonna speak Christian, then walk Christian. BE-LIVING CHRISTIAN!

The word of the day is "CHRISTIAN".

Matthew 25:31-46
John 13:34-35

Prayer - ♪♪Lord, I want to be a Christian in my heart, in my heart♪♪ (repeat as needed). In the name of Jesus, I pray. Amen. Amen. Amen.

Reflections: _____

_____

_____

_____

_____

_____

_____

_____

_____

_____

Applications: _____

_____

_____

_____

_____

_____

_____

_____

_____

THE WORD OF THE DAY IS "WHO"

Who created and controls all things? Who is the Alpha and the Omega, the beginning and the end? Who gives sight to the blind and hearing to the deaf? Who is a mother to the motherless and a father to the fatherless? Who can renew ruptured relationships and make them whole again? Who can make terminal illnesses temporary? Who is strong in our weakness? Who can open and close doors that no one else can? Who can make it rain across the street and have sunshine over your head? Who cares when no one else does? Who loves you unconditionally? Who forgives you every time you ask? Who declares to be with you always? Who, you ask? GOD, that is who! Who will you choose to serve?
The word of the day is "WHO".

Isaiah 40:28-31
John 8:25
Acts 9:5

Prayer - God, You are the one who is the source of all that I need. In the name of Jesus, I pray. Amen. Amen. Amen.

Reflections: _____

_____

_____

_____

_____

_____

_____

_____

_____

Applications: _____

_____

_____

_____

_____

_____

_____

_____

_____

THE WORD OF THE DAY IS "RELATIONSHIPS"

Relationships are a vital part of living; just as exercising and healthy eating are to being physically fit. Everyone, believe it or not, falls in one or more of the following relationship categories: acquaintances, associates, assignments, advisors and friends. Relationships worth having demand attention, communication and effort. Creating, maintaining and growing authentic relationships is an intentional and deliberate act. Sometimes relationships hurt. Most times relationships make us feel good; this, however, is not an indicator that the relationship is healthy. When relationships hurt, this is a sign that something needs to be shifted, changed or eliminated. Jesus is the master of relationships. He teaches us to engage with one another with humility, gentleness, patience, acceptance, love and peace regardless of the category one finds themself. The word of the day is "RELATIONSHIPS".

Ephesians 4:1-5
1 Peter 4:8

Prayer - Lord, I want to be in the right relationship with you, so that I can be in the right relationship with others. In the name of Jesus, I pray. Amen. Amen. Amen.

Reflections: _____

_____
_____
_____
_____
_____
_____
_____
_____

Applications: _____

_____
_____
_____
_____
_____
_____
_____
_____
_____

THE WORD OF THE DAY IS "SENT"

The word sent carries authority and purpose. No one is sent anywhere without an agenda to accomplish. The one sent is privileged by the authority of the sender. God sent His Son, Jesus. Jesus sent His disciples and further sends all who believe. Oftentimes we forget why we are sent, which is to make disciples for Jesus. Remember that although we are sent, we are not alone. Jesus sent the Holy Spirit to dwell in us, thereby the God the Father and Son are with us as we go.

The word of the day is "SENT".

Matthew 28:19-20
Mark 16:15

Prayer - Send me as you have been sent, Jesus. I will go! In the name of Jesus, I pray. Amen. Amen. Amen.

Reflections: _____
_____
_____
_____
_____
_____
_____
_____
_____
_____

Applications: _____
_____
_____
_____
_____
_____
_____
_____
_____

THE WORD OF THE DAY IS "WORK"

God is at work in the world, believe it or not! Look around you. If you are getting answers to prayer directly, that's God at work. If you experience or witness unexplained calmness amid hostility, that is nothing short of God at work. If you have experienced an event that you did not understand or it surpassed your own ability, that is God at work. You know God is at work when the power and wisdom of humanity have no explanation. Jesus is still calming storms, dining with sinners and rising in us all! God will meet you wherever you are and work in and through you for His glory. Take note and be more observant to what is happening around you and see the mighty hand of God at work.

The word of the day is "WORK".

Psalm 90:17
Habakkuk 1:5
Ephesians 4:28

Prayer - I know you are at work around me, Lord. Do a work in and through me. In the name of Jesus, I pray. Amen. Amen. Amen.

Reflections: _____
_____
_____
_____
_____
_____
_____
_____
_____
_____

Applications: _____
_____
_____
_____
_____
_____
_____
_____
_____

THE WORD OF THE DAY IS "PRAISE"

Praise be to God in the highest, for He is worthy to be praised! Amid a world filled with disgust, deceit, dysfunction, disease and death it is difficult to praise. One finds it easier to give God praise when winning at life. I submit to you that praise given in times of despair is far greater. Despite the trials and tribulations, we will experience, God is still worthy of all praise! He promises blessing, faithfulness, love, wholeness, abundance, strength and sufficient grace. Like Habakkuk, when everything around us seems to fail us, God never fails. Rejoice and give praise for the salvation of the Lord! Give God praise in all situations and circumstances!

The word of the day is "PRAISE".

Psalm 145:3
Isaiah 25:1
Habakkuk 3

Prayer - I praise you in the morning, noonday and in the evening. You deserve to be praised. In the name of Jesus, I pray. Amen. Amen. Amen.

Reflections: _____

_____
_____
_____
_____
_____
_____
_____
_____

Applications: _____

_____
_____
_____
_____
_____
_____
_____
_____

THE WORD OF THE DAY IS "OBEDIENCE"

We do not always like the direction God tells us to go. Yet, He patiently waits for us to respond in obedience. Unfortunately, we attempt to wait God out by doing nothing, hoping that God will speak to us again and tell us something different. Jonah found himself in the belly of a whale for his disobedience before being rewarded for his obedience the second time. Jeremiah received more revelation of God's plan and experienced greater blessing for being obedient the first time. I am glad that I serve a God of second chances! If you are waiting to hear from God, reflect on what He has already told you. Chances are His word for you is still the same. Do not waste your second chance. His blessing is waiting for you!

The word of the day is "OBEDIENCE".

Exodus 19:5-6
Jonah 1-3
John 15:9-10

Prayer - Lord give me the courage and confidence to take you at Your word the first time. In the name of Jesus, I pray. Amen. Amen. Amen.

Reflections: _____
_____
_____
_____
_____
_____
_____
_____
_____
_____

Applications: _____
_____
_____
_____
_____
_____
_____
_____
_____

THE WORD OF THE DAY IS "SPIRIT"

The Spirit of the living God resides in everyone who believes that Jesus died, was buried and raised from the grave. The Spirit of God is our advocate, adviser and comforter until Jesus returns. One has direct access to the Creator God because His very Spirit lives on the inside of us. God speaks to us through His Spirit. Moreover, it is through the Spirit of God that we experience an intimate relationship with Him. The Spirit reveals to us God's plan for our lives. If it is a revelation in your life that you seek, then become humble and obedient to God's word, God's will and God's way. The Spirit of God within you is waiting to be activated to reveal God's plan for your life.

The word of the day is "SPIRIT".

Job 33:4
Luke 11:9-13
John 4:24

Prayer - Fill me anew with your Spirit, God. I want You to be active on the inside of me. Let others see You when they see me. In the name of Jesus, I pray. Amen. Amen. Amen.

Reflections: _____
_____
_____
_____
_____
_____
_____
_____
_____
_____

Applications: _____
_____
_____
_____
_____
_____
_____
_____
_____
_____

THE WORD OF THE DAY IS "SERVE"

In John 21 Jesus asks Peter three times if he loved Him. This line of questioning is about Peter's denial of Jesus. Jesus then implored him, "If you love Me, feed My sheep" (v. 17). Our love for Jesus is shown, not only by our words, but by how we serve others. Jesus came to seek and save those who are lost, which means serving the lost, the lonely and the left behind - not by serving oneself, taking one's own interest and making them His. One can get caught up in doing so many things that have the appearance of loving Jesus, but do not serve Him or others at all. Jesus said that, "He came to serve, not be served." As a Christian, serving others becomes our priority.

The word of the day is "SERVE".

Joshua 24:15
Matthew 20:28
Luke 4:8

Prayer - I want to serve you more. Show me how I can serve others in your name, O God. In the name of Jesus, I pray. Amen. Amen. Amen.

Reflections: _____

_____
_____
_____
_____
_____
_____
_____
_____
_____

Applications: _____

_____
_____
_____
_____
_____
_____
_____
_____
_____

THE WORD OF THE DAY IS "PRAYER"

Prayer is a spiritual way Christians change the natural outcomes of life. Prayer is how humanity communicates with its Creator, God. The Bible teaches us to "pray without ceasing." Abraham prayed for 13 years that his son Ishmael would be different from his natural destiny. I do not know how long my father prayed that I would break the cycle of my natural self. The point is this: never give up on prayer! Be encouraged and willing to participate in the answer to your prayer. The answers do not always come when or how we want them. However, the answer is always timely, in God's perfect time. He is always on time!

The word of the day is "PRAYER".

Jeremiah 29:12
1 Thessalonians 5:17
1 John 5:14-16

Prayer - I want to talk with you more. God, I know you hear me. Speak to me in ways that I understand. In the name of Jesus, I pray. Amen. Amen. Amen.

Reflections: _____
_____
_____
_____
_____
_____
_____
_____
_____
_____

Applications: _____
_____
_____
_____
_____
_____
_____
_____
_____

THE WORD OF THE DAY IS "LABORERS"

It appears that there is always more work to do than there are laborers to do. The wealthy are quick to write a check. Others have someone else they can call if necessary. Few, however, are willing, accessible and available laborers. Consider this, Jesus could have spread the Good News all by Himself, but He did not. He chose a few ordinary men for an extraordinary mission and special work of discipleship. We are all called to co-labor with Jesus, as well, in spreading the Good News that the Kingdom of God is at hand. When one presents oneself as an accessible and available laborer before God, He will place you in position to gather His harvest. The harvest is truly plentiful, yet the laborers remain few. Do not let your labor be in vain.

The word of the day is "LABORERS".

Matthew 9:35-38
Luke 10:2

Prayer - Use me God, how you see fit and for your glory. Let my labor not be in vain. In the name of Jesus, I pray. Amen. Amen. Amen.

Reflections: _____
_____
_____
_____
_____
_____
_____
_____
_____
_____

Applications: _____
_____
_____
_____
_____
_____
_____
_____
_____

THE WORD OF THE DAY IS "PROVISION"

Kingdom building can be challenging. Just ask Elijah. He became overwhelmed and lost focus of God while in the presence of God's enemies. He felt exhausted, discouraged and alone. God came to him and gave him the provision of rest, peace and courage. God is "Jehovah Jireh". God has unfathomable provisions in the now and He will provide and prepare you for whatever is next in your life. God knows what you need before you ask. He knows how to care for and encourage you. God will never leave you alone. God's provision is plentiful and available for all who trust in Him.

The word of the day is "PROVISION".

Genesis 22:14
1 Kings 19
2 Corinthians 9:8

Prayer - You never fail to provide wherever you guide. God, I trust in your provision. In the name of Jesus, I pray. Amen. Amen. Amen.

Reflections: _____

_____

_____

_____

_____

_____

_____

_____

_____

_____

Applications: _____

_____

_____

_____

_____

_____

_____

_____

_____

THE WORD OF THE DAY IS "BATTLE"

Life's battles can be overwhelming. God promises that if we trust and obey Him, we will be victorious. On the contrary, if we turn away from Him and disobey His word, we will experience defeat. We can learn this lesson from the children of Israel. Because of their disobedience it took them forty years to reach the promised land instead of God's intended eleven days. The children of Israel allowed the difficulty to distract them from their destiny. The battles of life are oftentimes long and arduous but with God the victory remains ours. Do not give up or give in to the detours! You do not have to face the battle alone. When the battles seem too big, self-examine your heart and surrender to God. Ultimately the battle belongs to Him! Be aware that one's heart does not shift away from God during the battle. He will see you through.

The word of the day is "BATTLE".

Exodus 14:14
Deuteronomy 28
Ephesians 6:12

Prayer - God, I give you what is rightfully yours. Take this battle from me. In the name of Jesus, I pray. Amen. Amen. Amen.

Reflections: _____

_____
_____
_____
_____
_____
_____
_____
_____
_____

Applications: _____

_____
_____
_____
_____
_____
_____
_____
_____

THE WORD OF THE DAY IS "LIVE"

To live a life in the likeness of Christ is not easy. One is encouraged to be aggressive, steadfast and audacious in one's pursuit of righteous living. One will be challenged, discouraged and knocked down along the way. Paul warns Timothy that those who desire to live like Christ will suffer persecution. Christ, Himself, tells us in the gospel of John that, "the world hated Me for no reason. Surely they will hate those who follow after Me." The good news is this, although Christ was hated, persecuted and crucified He DID NOT stay dead. He was RAISED from the dead with ALL power in heaven and on earth in His hands! As a Christian we access that same power, that resurrection power, to live our lives more abundantly through the Holy Spirit living on the inside of us. Do you want to live abundantly?

The word of the day is "LIVE".

John 15:18-27
Romans 8:10-11
2 Timothy 3:10-17

Prayer - I live because the power of your Holy Spirit lives in me. Thank you for life, God. In the name of Jesus, I pray. Amen. Amen. Amen.

Reflections: _____

_____
_____
_____
_____
_____
_____
_____
_____
_____

Applications: _____

_____
_____
_____
_____
_____
_____
_____
_____
_____

THE WORD OF THE DAY "THINK"

Too often thought is not given its due respect. Both speech and action are usually impacted positively when thought is given beforehand. Think means to spend time processing and in contemplation about something or someone. The mind is a powerful organ, the thoughts developed by it shape who we are and what we become. "As we think, we change the physical nature of our brain. As we consciously direct our thinking, we can wire out toxic patterns of thinking and replace them with healthy thoughts." By changing the way, you think, you can change what you think, which can change your perspective and consequently can change how you act in the world. Therefore, every action reflects your thinking or lack thereof. Learn how to think. Be careful not to be told what to think. The word of the day is "THINK".

Proverbs 23:7
Colossians 3:2
1 Peter 1:13

Prayer: God let my thoughts be your thoughts and my ways be your ways. I want to think on heavenly things. In the name of Jesus, I pray. Amen. Amen. Amen.

Reflections: _____

_____

_____

_____

_____

_____

_____

_____

_____

Applications: _____

_____

_____

_____

_____

_____

_____

_____

_____

THE WORD OF THE DAY IS "PRAY"

It is customary to pray when you are desperate and in despair, seeking answers and intervention from God. The fact of the matter is that God knows your circumstances before you pray. He always answers prayer. However, the better question is, is anyone listening for God to answer? Not for what one wants to hear but for the voice of God that can be soft and tender, loud and booming or come from the least expected people and places. It is difficult for one to hear God when you pray during the hustle and bustle of life. Pray in a quiet, private place. One hears Him best in silence. One can receive answers and directions for the way forward amid silence when they pray.

The word of the day is "PRAY".

Matthew 6:6-13
Mark 11:24-25
1 Thessalonians 5:16-18

Prayer - Hear me throughout the day, O God. I cry out to you when in need and when supplied. In the name of Jesus, I pray. Amen. Amen. Amen.

Reflections: _____
_____
_____
_____
_____
_____
_____
_____
_____
_____

Applications: _____
_____
_____
_____
_____
_____
_____
_____
_____

THE WORD OF THE DAY IS "KNOW"

It is slanderous and dishonoring to serve God without knowing Him. Think about it for a second... when someone tries to make another happy and does not know what makes the other happy it is impossible. The challenges in the valleys of life will separate one from truly knowing God. It should be noted that without faith, it is indeed impossible to know God. When we go through the trials and tribulations of life, knowing God gives one confidence and courage that He will be present with them in the storm. Trusting God's word and consistent prayer leads one to know that they can do all things through Jesus, His Son.

The word of the day is "KNOW".

Isaiah 40:28
John 17:3
Philippians 4:13

Pray - I want to know you God, as you know me. Take my hand and show me your ways. In the name of Jesus, I pray. Amen. Amen. Amen.

Reflections: _____
_____
_____
_____
_____
_____
_____
_____
_____
_____

Applications: _____
_____
_____
_____
_____
_____
_____
_____
_____

THE WORD OF THE DAY IS "MOUNTAINTOP"

Everyone wants to have a mountaintop experience. However, the mountaintop is not for everyone. Jesus only took three of His twelve disciples to the mountaintop with Him. It is always an awesome experience to be on the mountaintop. The mountaintop, however, can cause one to become lackluster in their expressions of love, faithfulness and gratitude. That rarely happens in the valley. The valley is where the rigors of life challenge one's faith, where sickness and disease try to conquer and destroy them, and where the selfishness of humanity oppresses and blames each other for their shortcomings. Being in the valley of the shadow of death can cause one to become humble. However, the awesome power of the Holy Spirit reminds one to never fear. The goodness and mercies of God will follow one to again experience the mountaintop.

The word of the day is "MOUNTAINTOP".

Isaiah 52:7
Nahum 1:5
Matthew 17:1-8

Prayer - Teach me, Lord, in the valley how to best respond to the mountaintop. In the name of Jesus, I pray. Amen. Amen. Amen.

Reflections: _____

_____

_____

_____

_____

_____

_____

_____

_____

_____

Applications: _____

_____

_____

_____

_____

_____

_____

_____

_____

_____

THE WORD OF THE DAY IS "RUN"

Running can be misunderstood to become hasty. I submit to you: run with conviction, determination and excellence. Let all that you do be pleasing to God! The Bible teaches that one is to run the race that is before them. Some only run for a temporary crown; as a Christian, one runs for a crown that lasts forever. Do not be fooled by people that say, "You have been saved so it does not matter what you do." They are sadly mistaken! HOW you do WHAT you do reflects WHO you are. Run with a sense of immortality. When one's race is over how will the race run be remembered, or will it be remembered at all?

The word of the day is "RUN".

1 Corinthians 9:24-26
Hebrews 12:1-2
1 John 2:16-17

Prayer - Lord, help me run my race to the best of my ability and for your glory. In the name of Jesus, I pray. Amen. Amen. Amen.

Reflections: _____
_____
_____
_____
_____
_____
_____
_____
_____
_____

Applications: _____
_____
_____
_____
_____
_____
_____
_____

THE WORD OF THE DAY IS "TRUST"

It is difficult to trust what one does not know or is unfamiliar with. However, I am taken aback by how much trust is given with little thought or investigation. Consider then, trust to be something that can be lost not earned. Trust is typically a given until there is a reason or event that jeopardizes that trust. We often experience disappointment and disgust because of who and what we put our trust in. Trust comes through knowledge. Know God. When you put your trust in God you will experience His unconditional and unlimited love, grace, mercy and so much more.

The word of the day is "TRUST".

Psalm 56:3-4
Isaiah 40:29- 31
Jeremiah 17:7-8

Prayer - Lord, I will trust you, in all things! In the name of Jesus, I pray. Amen. Amen. Amen.

Reflections: _____
_____
_____
_____
_____
_____
_____
_____
_____

Applications: _____
_____
_____
_____
_____
_____
_____
_____
_____

THE WORD OF THE DAY IS "WAITING"

The act of waiting has become lost, archaic or otherwise taboo as our society has become riddled with a "right now" mentality. Technology has its benefits; encouraging one to wait is not one of them. What does one do "right now" when advised, told and ordered to "wait"? I have observed waiting turn into panic or anxiety. The art of waiting takes patience. Waiting involves praying, praising and preparing oneself to receive the goodness of a merciful and faithful God.

The word of the day is "WAITING".

Psalm 37:34
Lamentations 3:22-26
James 5:7-8

Prayer - Lord, I will praise you as I will wait for you. In the name of Jesus, I pray. Amen. Amen. Amen.

Reflections: _____

_____

_____

_____

_____

_____

_____

_____

_____

Applications: _____

_____

_____

_____

_____

_____

_____

_____

_____

THE WORD OF THE DAY IS "THANKFULNESS"

The attitude of thankfulness begins with humility. Thankfulness is an action taken in response to someone else's generosity, sacrifice and selflessness. Through prayer, reading God's word, living according to God's word and loving each other one shows thankfulness to the God of the universe who daily demonstrates His love, grace and mercy to everyone.

The word of the day is "THANKFULNESS".

Psalm 9:1-2
Philippians 4:6-7

Prayer - Thank you God for the air that I breathe, your love and your Son Jesus. In the name of Jesus, I pray. Amen. Amen. Amen.

Reflections: _____
_____
_____
_____
_____
_____
_____
_____
_____
_____

Applications: _____
_____
_____
_____
_____
_____
_____
_____
_____

THE WORD OF THE DAY IS "WEAKNESS"

It is difficult to acknowledge and admit one's weakness. Society teaches us to highlight our strengths and hide our weaknesses. By this, humanity becomes hyper focused on what it is good at while completely ignoring that which can be improved. Weakness is viewed as having less, saying less and doing less. Therefore, if one displays weakness, they are often devalued, silenced and set aside. In opposition to human thought, God finds weakness useful. His power is perfected and pronounced in one's weakness. When our weakness is abounding, God is strong! It is only in the weakness of humanity that the grace and power of God is revealed. The word of the day is "WEAKNESS".

Psalm 73:26
Romans 15:1
2 Corinthians 12:9-10

Prayer - You, O'God, are my strength when I am weak. Show yourself to me now. In the name of Jesus, I pray. Amen. Amen. Amen.

Reflections: _____
_____
_____
_____
_____
_____
_____
_____
_____
_____

Applications: _____
_____
_____
_____
_____
_____
_____
_____
_____

THE WORD OF THE DAY IS "STAMINA"

One of the keys to distance running is stamina. Stamina is both the energy and strength one has that allows them to sustain mental and physical effort for an extended amount of time. It can be especially difficult to maintain one's stamina during unpredictable and uncomfortable times. When one's stamina begins to wane, one must tap into someone one greater than themselves. I recommend Jesus. He neither sleeps nor slumbers. Through His strength one will be sustained. It does not take stamina to start anything, but stamina is necessary to finish. Jesus demonstrates stamina as the author and finisher of our faith. The word of the day is "STAMINA".

Psalm 30:1-5
Romans 5:3-4
Hebrews 10:35-36

Prayer - Help me Lord to finish better than I started, all to your glory. In the name of Jesus, I pray. Amen. Amen. Amen.

Reflections: _____

_____
_____
_____
_____
_____
_____
_____
_____

Applications: _____

_____
_____
_____
_____
_____
_____
_____
_____

THE WORD OF THE DAY IS "FOCUS"

The details of life are missed due to the lack of focus. Focus gives vision the necessary steps to become a reality. It is common for one to miss out on what is best because of a fickle focus. A spinning ballet dancer must continually return their eyes to a given focal point to maintain balance. Otherwise, they become unstable and flounder. Likewise, all of humanity must focus their eyes to its author and creator to sustain abundant living. When one's focus is on the Father, they experience an infinite future. The word of the day is "FOCUS".

Proverbs 4:25
2 Corinthians 4:18
Isaiah 50:7

Prayer - God, I you are the center of my joy. Therefore, all I think, do and say begins and ends with you. In the name of Jesus, I pray. Amen. Amen. Amen.

Reflections: _____
_____
_____
_____
_____
_____
_____
_____
_____
_____
_____

Applications: _____
_____
_____
_____
_____
_____
_____
_____
_____

THE WORD OF THE DAY IS "PERSPECTIVE"

One may be familiar with the truth that "one person's trash is another's treasure" or the sage wisdom, "change your perspective, change your world." There will always be a choice to make on how one looks at any given situation or circumstance. The way one looks at any given situation can be uplifting or downtrodden. The choice is yours! The people of Israel grumbled and complained while in the wilderness despite God's daily provisions. Some would have rather returned to slavery in Egypt with the knowledge of their limitations than to be free unaware of their limitless God. Seeing from an eternal perspective will change your life from famine to feast.

The word of the day is "PERSPECTIVE".

Colossians 3:2
1 John 4:4-6
1 Thessalonians 5:8-10

Prayer - God help me to see your goodness and your glory during tough times. In the name of Jesus, I pray. Amen. Amen. Amen.

Reflections: _____
_____
_____
_____
_____
_____
_____
_____
_____
_____

Applications: _____
_____
_____
_____
_____
_____
_____
_____
_____

THE WORD OF THE DAY IS "HAPHAZARD"

Haphazard is the absence of order or planning; not having a particular focus. It is a random reaction dependent or determined by chance; aimless. The rambunctious of humanity is a replication of a haphazard system that continues to resist and refuse change. There is a way out of haphazard living, decision making and action, it is called repentance! Repentance can realign one's relationship with God and fellowship with others. Change without purpose and intent is haphazard. God is purposeful and intentional. Through the power of God that resides in every Christian regardless of tradition, the haphazardly can be subsided. God is bigger, greater and stronger than any and everything. Do not become like those that encounter change through senseless, haphazard reactions, but take a direct and deliberate response that is God focused. The word of the day is "HAPHAZARD".

Isaiah 30:18-19
Timothy 2:3-6
2 Peter 3:9

Prayer - May all I think, say and do intentionally bring you glory, O God. In the name of Jesus, I pray. Amen. Amen. Amen.

Reflections: _____

_____
_____
_____
_____
_____
_____
_____
_____
_____

Applications: _____

_____
_____
_____
_____
_____
_____
_____
_____

THE WORD OF THE DAY IS "RELAX"

I am sure one finds it extremely difficult to relax amid the financial and economic uncertainty and pulverizing politics that is now negatively impacting the progress against the current pandemic. Although relax means to become less rigid, strict or tense, it does not mean to abandon or abolish discipline and responsibility. The most productive thing anyone can do right now is relax. Take some deep breaths, allow disappointment, hurt and pain to be released in the exhale; relax. Repeat slowly, if necessary. Higher levels of creativity, decision making, and innovation can be reached when one relaxes. Throughout the Bible, whenever angels appeared to someone, they greeted them with, "Relax". God is near and in control. Get out of His way and let Him work.

The word of the day is "RELAX".

Psalm 46:10
Psalm 61:1-4
Psalm 127:1-2

Prayer - (Take 3 deep breaths) God, I give you all my disappointment, hurt and stress. I will relax, knowing that you are in control of all things. In the name of Jesus, I pray. Amen. Amen. Amen.

Reflections: _____

_____
_____
_____
_____
_____
_____
_____
_____
_____
_____

Applications: _____

_____
_____
_____
_____
_____
_____
_____
_____
_____

THE WORD OF THE DAY IS "STILLNESS"

Something amazing, powerful and unexplainable happens during stillness. There is far greater activity when there is stillness. Do not mistake stillness for stagnation and slumber. There was stillness before the walls of Jericho came tumbling down. There was stillness before Gideon experienced victory over the Midianites. Jesus' stillness dispersed the Pharisees concerning the adulteress woman. Effectively employed stillness speaks far louder than clanging symbols, fire or gunshots! Stillness is a word in action. The fear of the enemy grows in stillness. A victim's voice is heard in stillness. Use stillness to educate yourself, collaborate with others and prepare to execute a well thought out plan that uproots evil and unites humanity. Stillness can be one's secret weapon. Speak loudly in stillness!

The word of the day is "STILLNESS".

Exodus 14:14
2 Chronicles 20:17
Psalm 37:37

Prayer - Help me be still, Lord. I pray for your mighty movement in my stillness. In the name of Jesus, I pray. Amen. Amen. Amen.

Reflections: _____
_____
_____
_____
_____
_____
_____
_____
_____
_____

Applications: _____
_____
_____
_____
_____
_____
_____
_____
_____

THE WORD OF THE DAY IS "CONFLICT"

Conflict is a struggle of opposing views within oneself or between others. Conflict is an inevitable necessity from which understanding, and unity emerge. Conflict is difficult and can be painful. However, going through conflict collectively, community can be achieved. The greatest conflict humanity faces are not with one another, but its Creator. Once humanity repents and reconciles with God, we receive the power to conquer the conflict within our communities.

The word of the day is "CONFLICT".

Proverbs 15:18
Matthew 5:23-26
Romans 12:17-21

Prayer - God, create in me a conduit spirit of community to serve those around me. In the name of Jesus, I pray. Amen. Amen. Amen.

Reflections: _____
_____
_____
_____
_____
_____
_____
_____
_____
_____

Applications: _____
_____
_____
_____
_____
_____
_____
_____
_____
_____

THE WORD OF THE DAY IS "REPENTANCE"

Repentance is a radical change of life, from one direction to another. Repentance is realigning oneself, however great or subtle, with God's intended plan. This means abandoning all that is outside the will, the way and the word of God. All have been called to turn from a way of living that leads to death. Instead, to follow the example of Jesus that leads to abundant life. Repentance begins with humility, giving and receiving forgiveness. Repentance continues with a conscious and deliberate awareness of one's attitude, actions and speech toward self and others. Change comes through repentance and everyone has an individual responsibility. Individual repentance is necessary to participate in community change.

The word of the day is "REPENTANCE".

2 Chronicles 7:14
Proverbs 28:13
Acts 17:30

Prayer - I acknowledge that I do not know or have all the answers, but God, you do. Show me your will and your way. I will follow you. In the name of Jesus, I pray. Amen. Amen. Amen.

Reflections: _____

_____
_____
_____
_____
_____
_____
_____
_____
_____

Applications: _____

_____
_____
_____
_____
_____
_____
_____
_____
_____

References

"Definition of Google | Dictionary.Com". www.Dictionary.Com, 2023, https://www.dictionary.com/browse/google.

"Dictionary by Merriam-Webster: America's Most-Trusted Online Dictionary". Merriam-Webster.Com, 2021, https://www.merriam-webster.com/.

HCSB Study Bible. Holman Bible Publishers, 2010.
Stanley, Charles F. Jesus, Our Perfect Hope. Thomas Nelson, 2018.
The Warrior's Bible. Life Publishers International, 2014.

The Wesley Study Bible, Common English Bible. Christian Resources Development Corporation, 2012.

ACKNOWLEDGEMENTS

Giving all glory and honor to God, first and foremost. Without His constant prompting I would have quit on this project a long time ago. Words cannot express the gratitude that fills my heart for the many people that were strategically placed in my path by God who encouraged me along the way.

Thank you and love you to the ends of the earth goes out to my bride and life partner, editor and broad-minded critic, who often sees what I cannot, Katie. You challenged me practically and theologically throughout this project. Your gracious and relentless support gave me space to write through the toughest moments of our life changes, community work, relocations and military training. Your constant calm amid the chaos is nothing short of the expression of the Holy Spirit within you. There are no adequate words to express my gratitude for you.

Thank you to both of my children, Michael and Esther for putting up with daddy's shenanigans and word play. You both inspired me to keep things simple and practical for even a child to understand. You helped me laugh at myself and find the joy and simple application in every "word" written.

Special thanks to my "Big Sis" Brita, barber Frank and fellow Army chaplain Bradley who directly and frequently asked and admonished me to write.

Special thanks to my mentors: Paul, Jim, Megan and Chaplain Foyou and my father who without a doubt believe in the giftings and anointing of God on my life.

Special thanks to my illustrator, Summer, for your timeliness and ability to articulate my words through art. You are the best and know me better than I thought you did.

To my brother in Christ, Bruce, who, other than my wife, has no problem telling me exactly what I do not want to hear. Yet, you always encouragingly challenge me to be all that God has called me to be - no holds barred. Thanks, brotha!

I want to give a huge shout out and thanks to Focus and Vision Ministries' first small group leader Sarah and intern Courtney. You both have been an affirmation and inspiration sent by God to motivate me to pour myself out into the next generation by speaking and living authentically, unapologetically and recklessly for Jesus.

Now, to my fellow chaplains from all branches of service and components, thank you for your advice, guidance and support. I hope I have represented you well and that you find this tool useful in your ministry as you advise, guide and care for the men and women on your watch.

Finally, to all the men and women who have and currently are serving our military, for being responsive and reciprocal as I offer to you what God has given me daily. You challenged me to be creative and consistent while bringing God to you and you to God. You motivate me! I will continue "Living the Call Fiercely; For God and country"!

I am overwhelmed with thanksgiving and love for everyone that has supported me past, present and future; to God be the glory!

www.ingramcontent.com/pod-product-compliance
Lightning Source LLC
Chambersburg PA
CBHW061731070526
44583CB00024B/3091